Maths makes the
world go round

Looking for learning in child led inquiry

by Kirstine Beeley

Cover design by Stephanie Breen
Book design by Design Dejour

Published by Playing to Learn - Kirstine Beeley www.playingtolearnuk.com

ISBN 978-0-9955315-2-9

Photography courtesy of Treehouse Pre-School, Winslow, Buckingham Park C of E Primary School, Aylesbury, Prestwood Primary School, Buckinghamshire and Essa Primary School, Bolton

Printed by Diverze Print Limited www.diverze.com
11 Ropa Court, Leighton Buzzard, Bedfordshire LU7 1DU

Printed in Great Britain

Although every precaution has been taken in the preparation of this book, the publisher and author assume no responsibility for errors or omissions. Neither is any liability assumed for damages resulting from the use of information contained herein.

With thanks to Louise Wetherall and Sarah Kingham for their patience in helping to edit the book and to all the staff and children at Treehouse Pre-School, without whom this book would not have been possible.

Contents

Introduction

Maths in early years is something I have had a personal passion for since my early teacher training days many, many years ago. I really believe that, as with other areas of good early years provision, the key to accessing learning is not in setting up specific, focused activities with limited learning objectives in mind, or worse, a photocopiable worksheet! I know from years of experience of working with children (young and older) that the way they learn best is by interaction with stimulating, exciting and engaging learning environments where they can follow their own learning path and develop their learning in their own, inspired ways.

With that in mind I have focused this book, like my others, on practical and affordable ideas of how you can boost the chances of maths making it into children's play. I have tried to show that maths can be accessed outdoors and indoors and that it isn't just about number lines everywhere! Maths truly is integrated into so many aspects of everyday life and it is this that we as practitioners need to learn to look for in children's play.

Maths as a subject goes far beyond just being able to count or "know your numbers". It is the means by which we function on a daily basis with everyday tasks. We use maths to measure everything from how much tea we put into our cups to how much pasta to use in our dinner. We use counting, addition, subtraction and multiplication everyday as we shop, bake, fill our cars with petrol, or pay the bills. Many practitioners I have had the fortune of working with over the years have lacked in confidence to explore a variety of maths content due partly to a lack of their own confidence and understanding. If we cannot understand the relevance of maths in everyday situations how can we encourage children to do so? For this reason, I have tried to include some explanation of the maths

processes involved in early play in the hope of dispelling some of the fear practitioners have with maths and hopefully showing that you are probably seeing loads of maths everyday but maybe not realising.

The key difference with child led early years inquiry as opposed to traditional "teach at" approaches is that the role of the adult in the process. Adults cease to be the centre of focus, the founts of all knowledge and the drivers of direction, and begin to become the supporters of children's interest, the scaffolders of ongoing exploration and the facilitators of learning. We as practitioners must learn to step back and look for the opportunities to sensitively support children and to build on what the children already know and understand. This has never been more important than in maths learning. It is vital to realise from the start that there is a huge difference between a child doing something correctly once or even twice, particularly when it comes to worksheets etc., and a child truly understanding the concept that they are exploring. Much of people's distaste for maths stems from a lack of understanding, rooted in having been made to do something that they never really understood the relevance of. In early years we have the opportunity to look for and show children the ways that maths is a part of everyday experiences and to build on their ability to not just repeat or regurgitate information for the sake of some timely box ticking but to give them a real understanding of the uses and relevance of maths in our wider world.

If you are looking for activities as a template or photocopiable resources this is definitely not the book for you. If however you, like me, are passionate about child led inquiry and looking for the learning potential in what children choose to explore then I really hope you enjoy this book as much as I have enjoyed writing it. As ever thanks to the teams at Treehouse and Buckingham Park for their support and unerring faith in me – I am proud to be viewed as part of your teams.

Kirstine ☺

Maths makes the world go around.....

Maths in Early Years

Central to both this book and my approach to maths in early years is the belief that maths is integral to many everyday play situations and that planning for maths to happen has to be viewed differently to traditional planning. For maths to become accessible we, as practitioners, need to move away from paper based planning formats and look to plan and develop environments which are rich with mathematical opportunity. Maths rich environments need to be exciting, stimulating and interesting in equal measure. We need to embrace a world where we look for the learning within what children choose to do and are excited about, rather than trying to force contrived activities upon them and then wondering why they do not engage with maths even from this early age.

Maths should never be viewed in insolation and should always be seen as integral to all provision both indoors and outdoors . Maths is not just something that happens at a "maths table". Children learn best when all of their senses are stimulated, building loads of new brain connections each time which will last a lifetime. With this in mind, we as practitioners need to think carefully about how maths exploration can be integrated into and built upon within multisensory provision. By its very nature this then means that maths becomes a part of all areas of learning within our setting.

Enabling Environments

If we are not planning specific tasks but developing our environments, then we need to look at our settings and make sure that they offer access, excitement and interest so that children are able to explore freely. All early years environments need to have resources accessible to children and lots of plastic trays does not always offer this. Rethinking how we display resources can have a huge effect on whether or not children engage with their surroundings. Smaller collections of resources in open baskets can allow children easier choice and the option to move their play to wherever they want. Maths resources therefore need to be offered openly around the setting and not just in one area. Sometimes storing some mathematical resources together can focus adult attention but there still needs to be other equipment around the setting and children need to be shown that they do not have to confine their mathematical exploration and problem

solving to just one place. As with other areas of learning in early years we need to ensure that there is both space and time for children to explore their own ideas. Do we have too much furniture that is stifling the type of play which is happening? Does a rigid timetable of assemblies, playtime and P.E. take away opportunities for children get really involved in their exploration and to see ideas through to natural conclusions? Do we encourage children to be independent in their choices instead of relying on us for activities and direction? For child led inquiry to really have impact all of these factors need to be considered.

Invitations to Play

Although we are not planning activities for any one maths concept, it does not mean that we cannot enhance our provision with "invitations to play". These are open ended enhancements that have the possibility of mathematical exploration, but equally could go down a number of different learning paths. These, in my opinion, are different to "adult led" activities where there are often narrow learning objectives and very little scope to build on other areas of learning. Sometimes it is worth reviewing an idea for an invitation and asking ourselves "does this give the children scope to explore and learn or is there only one way to use this?" (however visually appealing it might be and however long it took us to build it!). Open endedness is central to a good invitation to play. That and the adult's ability to shift their focus should a child decide to take the play in a completely unplanned direction!

Number

Not just numerals

Let's be clear from the off that number is so much more than just knowing the written form of a number (the numeral). It is not about just being able to count and it is definitely not about being able to write numbers. Writing numerals is a physical and writing skill and comes much further down the learning and development line. Number knowledge is about being able to understand that the word for a number represents a group of objects or an amount. Just because a child can count a set of objects once does not mean that they fully understand the concept of that number. Children need lots of opportunity to visit and revisit the various skills of counting within all areas of their play if they are to develop a true understanding of what number really is and how it applies to their everyday lives. It is also worth remembering that obvious repeatable patterns do not start to occur in counting until children reach the 20s.

Number rich environments/making maths relevant

With this in mind we as practitioners need to focus our efforts on developing a number rich environment rather than specific number activities. This does not mean that there are laminated numerals stuck to every flat surface or hanging from every ceiling hook. Doing the "number line limbo" to get across your class will not ensure that children automatically "know their numbers"! A number rich environment is one where there are opportunities to talk about, to explore and to investigate counting in all areas of play, not just on a "maths table". It is the difference between setting out a "counting activity" and resourcing your learning environment with a wide variety of open ended, exciting and sensory objects where there is potential but not prescription. Don't get me wrong, I don't mean you don't need any number lines, but I would urge you to make them relevant to the children. A number line made from birthday cards is so much more engaging for children than a laminated generic printed product. Our numeral offering needs to make sense to the children and therefore needs to reflect the many ways that numerals are part of our everyday routines and environments. Make sure you have lots of remote controls, calculators, mobile phones (real but not working), catalogues, TV guides, packets, tins, phone books, cookbooks, rulers, tape measures, watches, clocks, or calendars as part of your offering. They all offer numerals within a real life context.

Outdoor numeracy

Remember that outdoor learning is not indoor learning brought out through the door. It should reflect the outdoor environment and build on all that the space, nature and the elements can offer. Outdoor environments can offer loads of maths experiences that have their own uniqueness, and at the point of printing this book I am not yet aware of any trees or plants that grow laminated numbers! Nature itself has loads of chances to explore not just number and counting but all areas of maths. Throughout the book I will refer to these differences and ways that we can resource our outdoor spaces to make all areas of maths, not just number, accessible to children.

Counting

Counting as a learning process consists of many different skills for children to master. From being able to count out loud to counting the items in your shopping bag, the skills are very different and need to be resourced accordingly. Here, I hope to be able to break down these skills a little and to look at how they may impact on our resourcing of our settings.

Reciting and recalling

One of the first things children learn to do with numbers is to recite them in order. Being able to say 1,2,3,4,5 does not mean that they understand what each of the numbers is but is none the less a part of the number learning process. Obviously exposing children to loads of songs and rhymes which recite numbers in order is vital to this process. Developing story/ songs sacks with props that encourage children to sing counting songs is a great way to enhance your setting, especially if the children are allowed free access to it rather than waiting for the adult to decide when it is time to sing a song or recite a rhyme. As practitioners we need to be looking for every opportunity to count in order or to recite the number names in order. Leading by example in our use of number language will encourage children to do the same, so counting out loud at every opportunity is key. The more children hear the sounds of the numbers in order the more they will get to grips with the order. Young children often grasp the idea of counting out loud but not necessarily in order. How many times have you heard a child say 1, 2, 3, 16 ?! Praise their confidence to try counting and offer yourself as a role model. The children are learning that one word follows another and so on. It takes a while and an awful lot of exposure to counting for children to get to grips with the numbers always being in the same order.

As part of this reciting process where children are playing with number words we have to make sure that they have access to counting backwards as well as counting forwards. It is important to build up a bank of songs and rhymes that count backwards and which end up with zero. Using the word zero from the off is important and has an impact for future maths understanding, where empty set knowledge will become more and more important. Rhymes such as 'ten in the bed', 'monkeys jumping on the bed' and 'five little men in a flying saucer' all count backwards. Rhymes such as '1,2,3,4,5, ..once I caught a fish alive', 'one potato, two potato' and 'one, two buckle my shoe' count forwards.

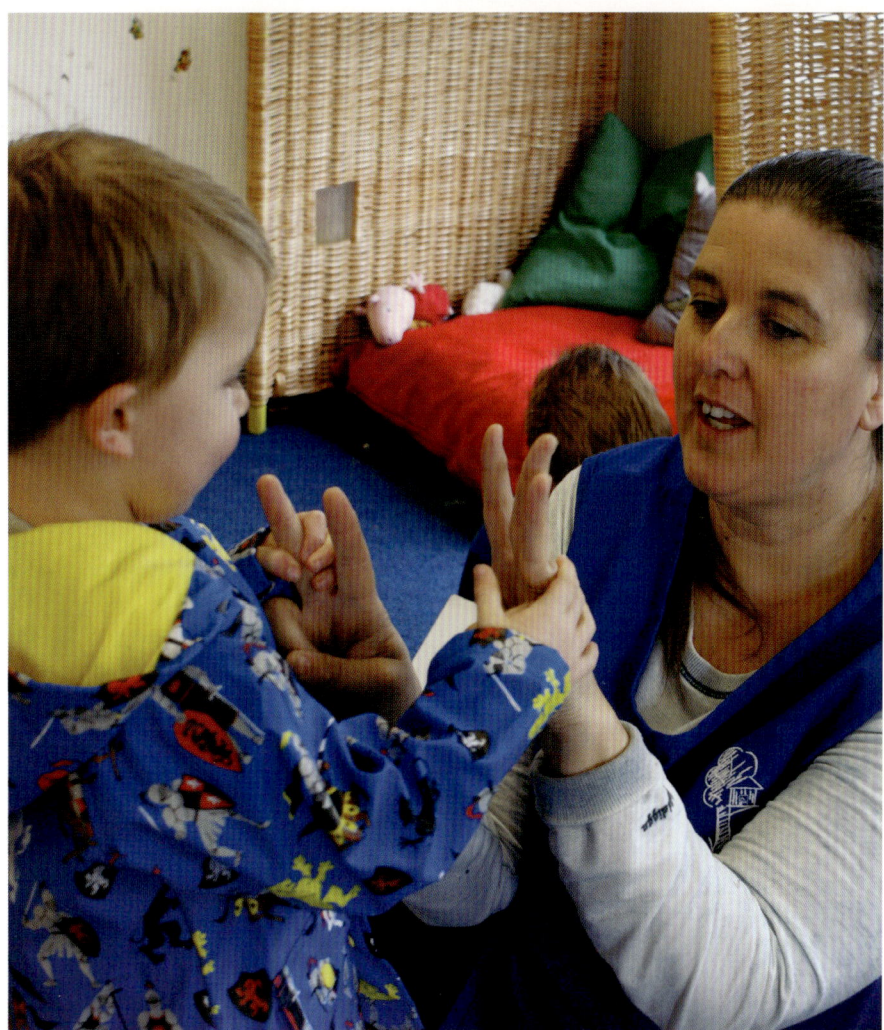

Moveable

Before children ever begin to explore the written form of number they have to get to grips with counting as a process. It is not as simple as once you can count you can count everything; there are different skills to master and understanding to gain. Within children's play look for opportunities to count anything that moves. Movable objects allow children to physically push one object as they say "one" and so forth, hence beginning to build up an understanding that the numbers refer to how many and that you give each object a number of its own and stop when you run out. Counting moveable objects very much depends on us enabling our environments with lots of interesting and exciting objects that could possibly be counted. Loose parts of all sorts both indoors and outdoors offer loads of opportunity for counting practice. Don't forget that the key to good child led learning is sensitive adult intervention so we need to be mindful of when we offer counting into the mix. Ploughing into the middle of imaginative story telling with "how many ponies do you have?" will usually only serve to end the play and send the child off in the opposite direction to you. We have to make sure we are involved in the play first and not trying to impose our own assessment criteria on the children's ideas.

Remember it is only with exposure to loads of counting objects that children will learn that the last number they get to represents the number of objects they have.

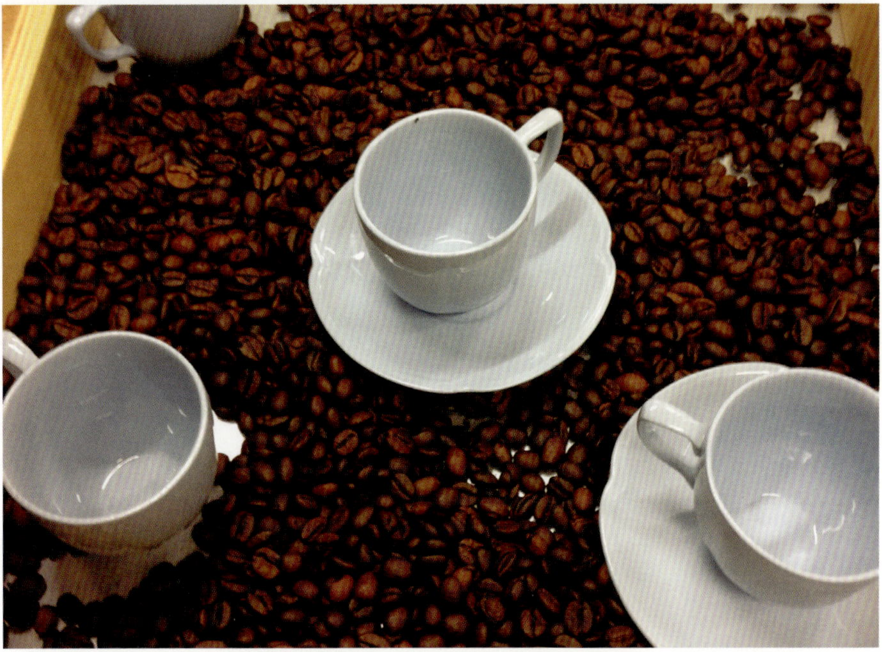

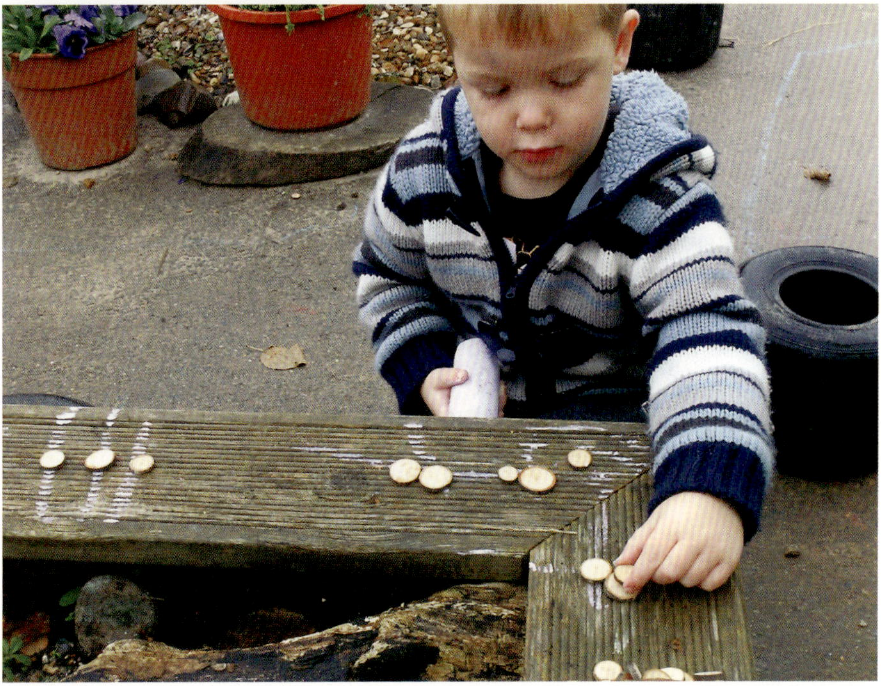

Non Moveable

The process of counting non-moveable objects is a very different skill. It involves the children being able to not only count one to one with the objects but also to remember where they started and to know when to stop. This is why for many children number lines and posters with sets of non moveable objects make little sense until they have been able to count moveable objects in loads of different play situations. Children really need to have mastered the skill of one to one counting before they can do this and the use of photocopiable sheets and worksheets seems of little use as an assessment of this skill before children have shown they are confident with counting loose parts. Many of the opportunities to count non-moveable objects such as dots on a ladybird or a dice, or the hearts on a playing card are not necessarily using this method of counting but are utilising a skill called "subitisation".

Subitising

Subitising is a complicated maths term for looking at a group of objects and being able to recognise how many there are without having to count each one. The skill is helped by familiar formations of objects – i.e. on dice and dominoes 5 is represented as four dots in a square with one more in the middle and children start to recognise this configuration and associate it with the number 5. It is what we do when we look at a dice or a domino and usually involves small numbers up to 5 or 6. As some children are naturally visual learners this is a method of building numerical skills that we need to nurture. We need to make sure that our environments are rich in resources that utilise this skill. Dominoes, dice, playing cards etc. are all everyday examples and having lots around helps children to be able to recognise a set of objects instantly. This is also the method children begin to use when looking at things like dots on ladybirds etc.

Name that number

As I have said before, recognising the written form of the number (the numeral) is a whole skill in itself and comes at a time when children are beginning to understand that marks carry meaning, developing alongside early letter understanding. It is important to separate the recognition of numerals from the skill of writing numerals as these are very separate skills, with the latter very much relying on children's physical development rather than their mathematical knowledge.

The skill of recognising numerals is made harder by the fact that very few numerals have anything about their form that relates to the amount they refer to. For example the number 5 has no notable reference to 5 objects and children will recognise representations such as 5 dots on a dice or 5 fingers long before they recognise the numeral.

This is why, as with all other areas of early years development we have to make numerals relevant to the children and their everyday lives. We should look at ways of using familiar numerals in our setting, for example birthday cards with numbers on or cake candles in the playdough with the numbers on. Resourcing our environments with these numerals will then allow children to explore those numerals of "personal significance" to them and you will find them saying things like "I am this" or "My sister is this many".

CHUNKY CANDLE
TESCO
0
CHUNKY CANDLE
TESCO
1
CHUNKY CANDLE
TESCO
2
CHUNKY CANDLE
TESCO
3
CHUNKY CANDLE
TESCO
4
CHUNKY CANDLE
TESCO
5

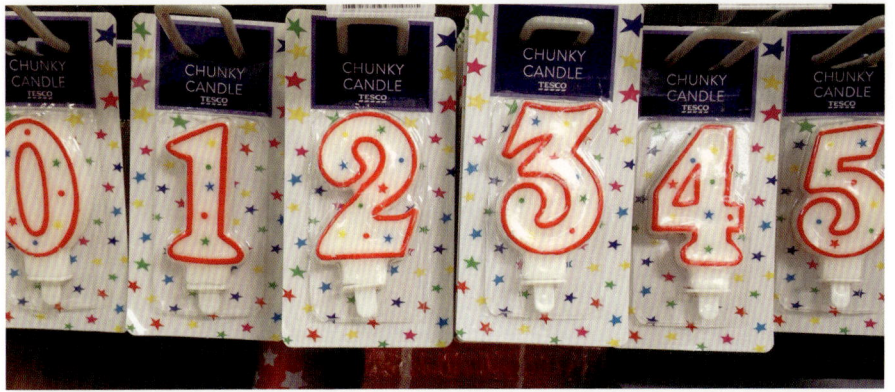

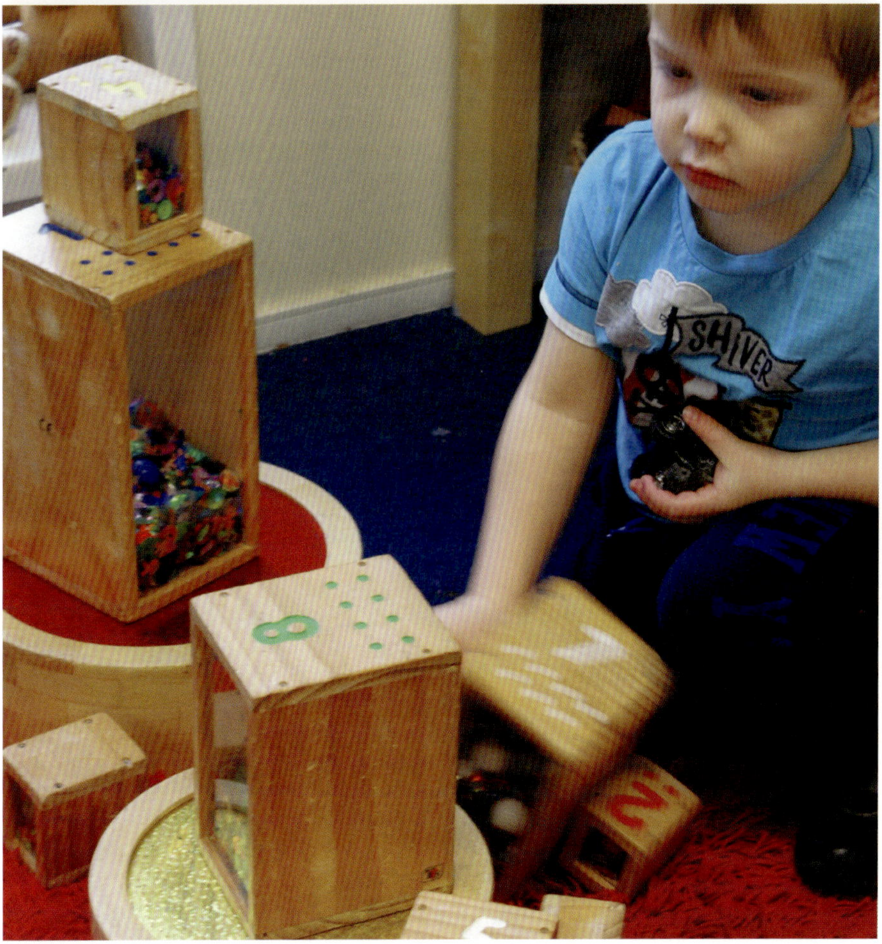
8

Number

We also need to make sure that we resource our settings with lots of numerals that are exciting, engaging and interesting and can be used as integral parts of the children's play. Just because you stick laminated numbers of starfish into the sand tray does not automatically mean the children will start talking about numerals as they scoop and fill! Try adding things like door numbers, raffle tickets, cake candles in the shape of numbers, birthday cards, birthday balloons, plastic magnetic numbers sprayed silver or gold, coins with numbers on, scallop shells and pebbles with numbers on etc. Be mindful that we are resourcing the environment for mathematical possibility not devising activities for the children to complete. We are just making sure that if an opportunity for counting and talking about numerals comes up in play we have an array of options to hand to help us scaffold and develop the children's existing learning.

Counting out

Once confident to count a set number of moveable objects with a one number one object method the next level of skill and understanding is to ask children to count out a certain number from a bigger set of objects. Asking them to count us out 5 pine cones or 3 cups takes maths skills on several levels. Children understand that they must have a certain number of objects to match the number you said, they know they have to count the objects out one at a time and they then have to understand that they stop once they have the right number. With such a complex process it is easy to see why enabling our environments with a wide variety of countable objects and opportunities is so important. Children must visit and revisit all of the aspects of this task separately before they will ever be able to put them together and even then will need lots of practice interacting with you to get the skill mastered.

The Language of More and Less

Once children are confident with counting objects we look at helping them understand the concept of one number being more or less than another. Quite a leap in skill and understanding I think you will agree? For children to even begin to make sense of this concept we have to return to the importance of language in maths and children's initial grasp of what more and less means long before they start to apply it to numbers. Exploring more and less with other aspects of maths helps children to really grasp the idea of more meaning you have a bigger quality of something. This language can easily be introduced to sand or water play, to mud kitchen cooking or to fine motor filling and scooping exploration. It is only when the terms more and less are explored with regards to visually obvious concepts such as sand, gravel, pinecones (without counting) etc. that children will stand a chance of transferring that understanding to the world of numbers.

Once they are happy with both terms and their relevance to quantity AND are happy with counting numbers of objects AND are able to order smaller numbers correctly, then they are able to begin to explore one number being more or less than the another. As with all the other aspects of number and counting we have to provide loads of exciting ways for children to explore our environments, with us looking for ways to introduce the mathematical language into the play without stifling the learning. Knowing that 5 is more than 3 is much easier to understand when you are talking about how many carrots to put in your magic stew in the garden than if you give a child a worksheet to complete. When exploring more and less do so more generally and very visually before you look at specifics such as one more or one less.

Addition, subtraction and all that Jazz!

Without being dismissive I could go on for ages breaking down the skills within addition, subtraction, halving, dividing, multiplying etc. However, if we have enabled our environments with lots of unique and engaging opportunities and resources that allow our children to explore the many aspects of counting within their own self led play and exploration, they will build confidence to count sets of objects and an understanding of what a number such as 5 really means (the fiveness of five). At which point we as practitioners do exactly what we have done with basic counting skills and look for opportunities to scaffold and expand maths knowledge further within play. Looking for chances to talk about sharing the objects in the mud kitchen between two saucepans or making sure we have enough sets of beads for each child who wants to thread them onto their spaghetti gives amazing ways of showing children the usefulness and relevance of these higher-level maths skills whilst still modelling the important maths language. As with all maths it is about the practitioner being confident in what they are looking at and taking chances to offer extensions to learning. More specific examples of what we can be looking out for come in the **Looking for Learning** section of this book.

Counting in twos

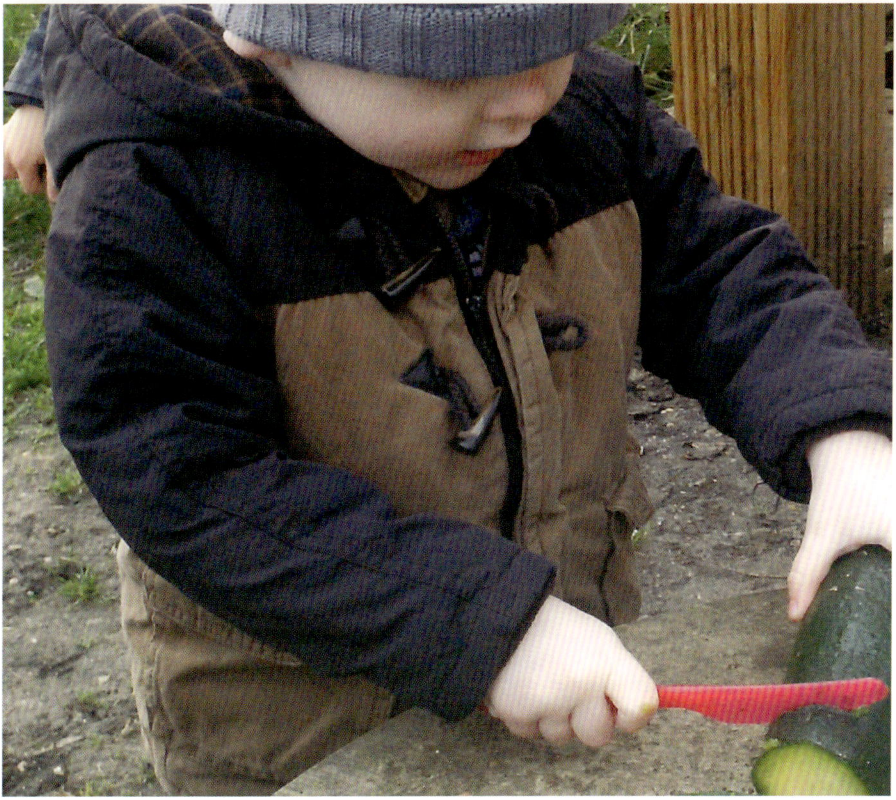

Sharing/division

Shape, space and measure

As with all areas of early maths the emphasis is on developing your environment and not on planning individual activities. For maths to make sense to children it needs to link with what the children are familiar with. Therefore, in this section we will be looking at not only what learning we as practitioners need to be looking for but how maths can be found in and around our settings if we have enabled them for maths potential.

enable ... excite ... engage ... explore

Shape

With shape there is often a tendency to focus on getting children to recognise and remember the names of regular 2 and 3 dimensional shapes such as triangles, circles and spheres. At an early age this memory testing is not a maths skill, just a test of visual recognition. What we do need to be doing is to build an environment which is rich in the language of shape. Where the use of shapes in and around us is recognised on a daily basis and the language is used by children and adults alike. The language of shape is not just about being able to explain the exact number of faces or vertices (the pointy corner bits!), it involves encouraging children to explore the use of language in describing all objects around them. It is very much linked to the sensory exploration of the environment and to the development of early language and communication skills. A child finding a snail in the garden might describe the shape as windy, wiggly or round and round – this is them using language to describe shape and should be encouraged. Yes, there is a place for talking about sides, edges, points, corners, vertices and faces but in early years we need to concentrate on the confidence to use any language to describe what they see and feel. It's worth remembering that as well as regular shapes such as squares, circles and triangles, the world if full of irregular shapes and children need to build their confidence to describe these too. Using words such as wiggling, curved, round, pointy and bumpy are all ways of describing shapes in our environments.

Environmental Shapes

As with all areas of best practice in early years, children learn and understand concepts best if they relate to their immediate environment or personal experiences. Shape is no different in this and we have to, as practitioners, become aware of the wide variety of shapes in and around our settings; allowing us to comment on them as part of children's own play rather than taking them all on a shape hunt when they have absolutely no interest or enthusiasm for looking for shapes. Take time to look around you for examples of circles, triangles, rectangles (oblongs) and squares (a special rectangle) as well as 3 dimensional shapes such as cylinders, cuboids and pyramids. Looking at your environment through a camera or tablet lens can help staff to see the wide variety of shapes both indoors and outdoors and to focus their attention on the potential for shape talk within children's play. If we have well-resourced creation stations and role play houses with lots of boxes, packets and tins, we have a readymade source of 3d shapes which actually have meaning to children. It is much easier for children to understand that a toothpaste tube is a cuboid and a baked bean tin is a cylinder.

Remember that being able to talk about shapes will go hand in hand with children's number skills and understanding. There is no point in asking a child how many sides a triangle has got if they aren't confidently counting moveable and non-moveable objects to 3!

Shape, Space & Measure

Sorting and Matching

The key to sorting and matching is the child's ability to be able to look at, and feel objects and to identify similarities and differences. Sorting objects according to differing attributes goes hand in hand with the development of shape language skills and shape recognition skills as well as developing comparison skills. Children need lots of opportunities to explore exciting and engaging materials and loose parts that have lots of sensory variety so that they can play with and talk about what makes them different and what is the same. Remember this has to occur as part of the child's ongoing play rather than us setting out a group of objects and asking children to sort according to colour or size etc. We as practitioners need to be looking for the process of sorting as children explore environments and then look for opportunities to scaffold and build on their existing language and understanding.

It is important to remember that children can sort according to any criteria they choose rather than one we choose for them. They may choose colour, size, shape or just to put all the horses together or separate all the cars from the lorries. The important skill is being confident in using language to explain their choices. If a child builds a set of objects and maintains that "they are the things I like", they are sorting according to a valid criteria.

Open ended resources

Sorting, along with counting, patterning and measuring, requires access to lots of loose parts with no right or wrong way to use them. This is essential if we are to unlock the maths potential within our environments. From a practitioner perspective, it requires a change to "traditional lesson planned" teaching approaches and asks that we take a step back and watch for chances to join in with play and enhance what the children have chosen to explore. With loose parts, both large and small, indoors and outdoors, the potential for maths language and exploration will naturally come hand in hand with other areas of development. Creativity, problem solving, early science and physical development skills all sit easily alongside sorting and matching skills, hence when observing children's play we have to be aware that we will probably be noting development in more than just one area of development. This differs from pre-planned, adult led activities where the focus will be on only one specific area of development and observations will concentrate on a can or cannot do basis. With child led learning, all children CAN DO, they just do it in their own way!

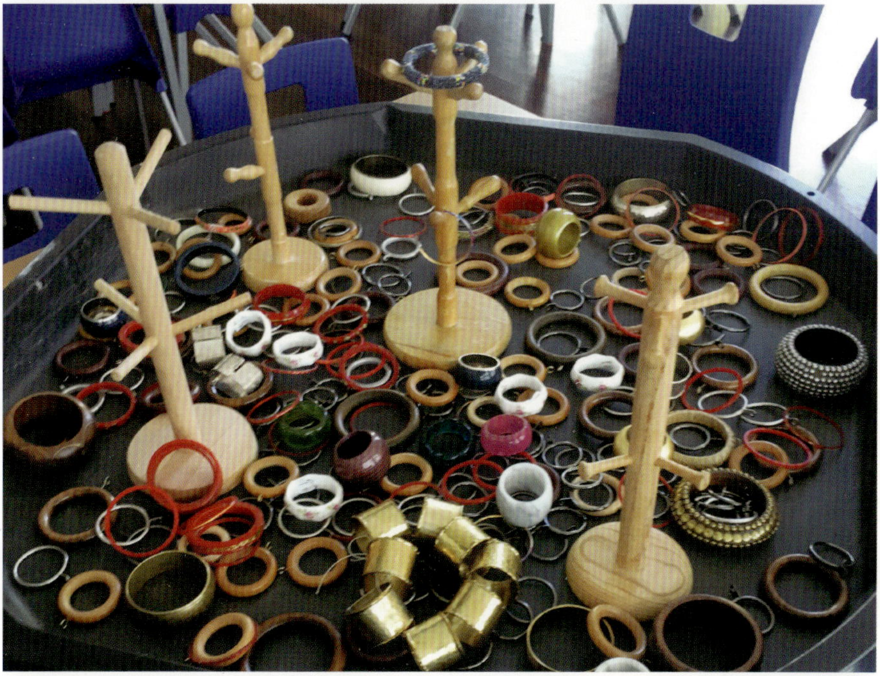

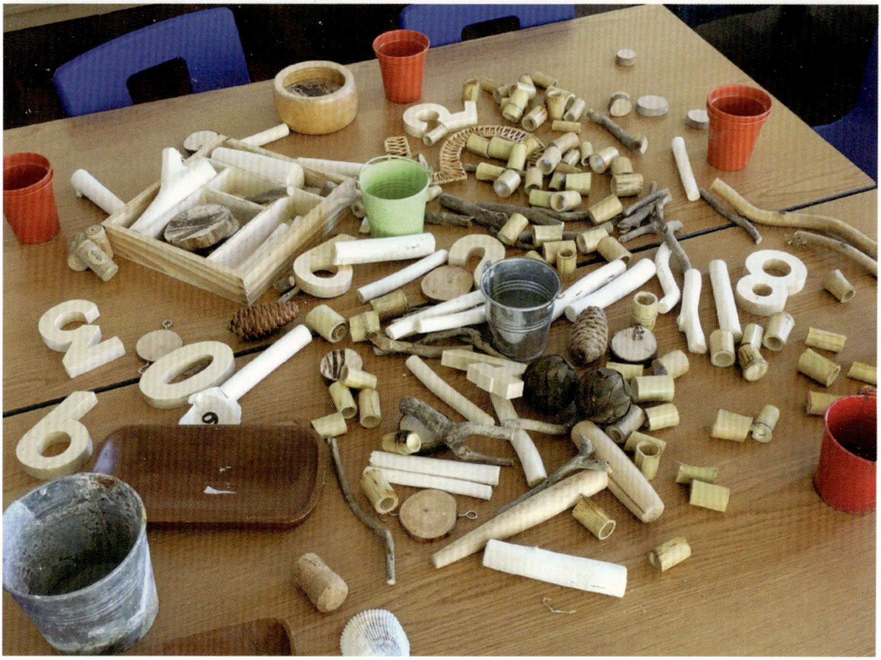

Patterns

Maths is all about patterns. Addition, subtraction, multiplication and division will all show patterns, tessellating shapes show patterns, counting is based on patterns (one more each time), counting in 2's, 5's and 10's is all about following a pattern. So we have to, from a very early age, encourage children to see the patterns in what they play with. The pattern can involve length, weight, capacity, shape, colour, patterns within patterns (spotty then stripy) or size. We must encourage our children to talk about their patterns when they build creations with loose parts, creative materials or even with pens or chalk. The idea with a pattern is that the same criteria are applied each time. Every pattern has an element of repetition but not always in a visual way. Patterns can be repeating colours or shapes or sizes (big, small, big, small etc.) or they can be increasing or decreasing patterns (big, bigger, even bigger, biggest). Patterns can involve shapes that fit together or rotate each time to make other shapes. The important skill is to help children recognise these patterns and eventually to be able to replicate or extend the patterns they choose to make. Don't forget to model maths language as you explore pattern with children as they play. Using words such as more, less, next, last, before and after is not only building patterning maths language but building on understanding key to early counting understanding too.

Space

Spatial awareness, like all other areas of maths, goes hand in hand with other areas of learning. In particular, it develops really closely alongside physical development. Children start to explore the world around them from birth and as such begin to explore not only how objects fit into their environment but also how they themselves do. Young children build their understanding of space around them and how they can fit in, under or through things at the same time as working out what fits where as they play with familiar objects. As practitioners, we need to look for opportunities to point this out within their play and exploration so that children build their understanding as part of what they are already doing, rather than it being an isolated skill planned as part of a laminated table top lesson. Providing an environment, which is rich in open ended objects that can be fitted together or where things can be put inside of other things, will hopefully stimulate inquiry and mathematical investigation. Including things such as puzzles, stacking activities, threading and posting resources builds both spatial awareness and fine motor co-ordination skills.

It is vital that we give children the opportunity to explore whole body movements to enable them to build their sense of their own personal space and how they function alongside other children, so resourcing our environments with this in mind is essential. Outdoor learning by its very nature gives children the chance to explore bigger spaces and to develop their awareness of their own bodies within those spaces. Filling your outdoor spaces with opportunities to brush, mop, swing, throw, jump, climb and spin will support this potential.

Bikes and trikes... or not?

When planning outdoor spaces we need to assess the skills and experiences we are offering our children and look at how these are helping them to grow in all areas of learning and personal confidence. With often limited spaces it may be worth asking whether or not the inclusion of bikes and trikes enhances these goals or interferes with it. Early Learning guidance such as the EYFS (DfE 2017) does not ask that children be able to ride bikes, but does ask that children build gross and fine motor skills, develop a sense of spatial awareness and are able to climb and step from one level to another. Sometimes removing bikes and trikes from an area can force the development of other learning opportunities which are much more wide-reaching than just turn taking and an awareness of speed (and why practitioners shouldn't wear open toed shoes!).

Positional Language

Environments rich in physical opportunity are key to developing not just children's use of positional language but their understanding of it. Children need the chance to be in, on, under, to climb through, leap off, stand next to and to be behind and in front of things. Creating spaces that children can go into not only develops their mathematical understanding but opens up lots of chances to talk and explore language with their peers.

Outdoor learning obviously plays a huge part in developing positional language mastery but only if the environment has been developed with these skills in mind. Do we have spaces that children can crawl through or in to? Can they climb along, step up, jump off, crawl under or roll down? An environment with lots of levels can be both easy to achieve and very empowering for children. Providing levels for children to climb up, jump off or sit on does not need to be confined to outdoors either. Try adding some extra levels indoors too and see how much children embrace the physical challenge as well as the maths language. Positional language in maths is therefore about really experiencing first hand next to, on top of, under etc. rather than sitting with a toy bear and a chair and putting him somewhere following an adult's instruction. Children really need to live the maths to learn it.

Measure

Measuring in early years draws on all of the previous maths skills discussed in the book so far. It draws on counting skills, number skills, comparison skills and co-ordination skills. Measuring isn't just about how long something is; it covers key areas of mathematical measurement such as length, weight, capacity, time and money. All of these need lots of play experience for them to begin making any sense to the children. Also the language of maths has to be central to developing their understanding of these maths concepts.

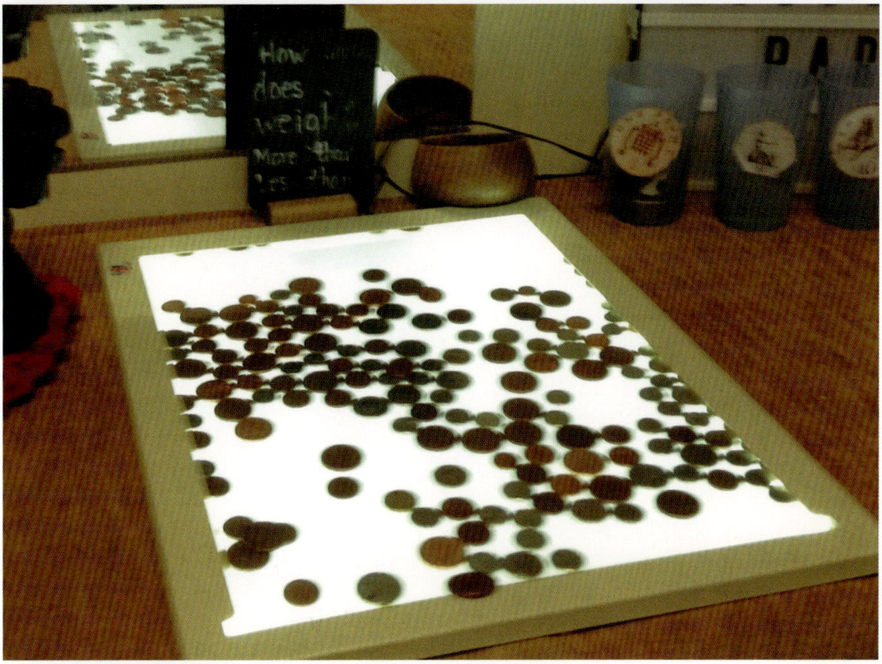

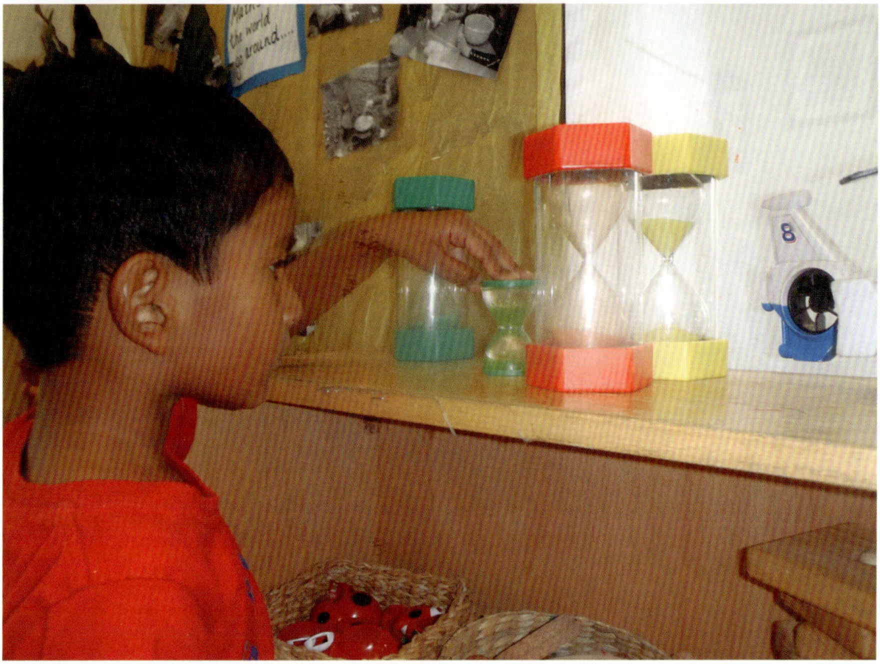

Language of Learning

Being confident in what language to use when you are playing with children as they pour water, scoop sand or pile conkers and apples onto the scales is essential for children's learning to develop. Adults have to know what words and terminology to use as they play alongside the children. My advice is always to sit as a team and brainstorm all of the language you want to be using to draw out maths understanding in the different areas of measurement and then to display them somewhere above child height so that staff can use them as prompts as they play. A kind of word wall for the workers! This way all staff know and agree what terminology will be used and have the benefit of an environment which not only supports the children's learning but their own mathematical understanding. A table of maths language is included on the next page to help you start this process.

Language of Maths

Number

Number, zero, none, nothing, one, two, three... to twenty and beyond

How many?, more, less, the same as, one more, one less,

Odd, even

Count, count (up) to, count on (from, to), count back (from, to)

Count in ones, twos, fives, tens

Few, fewer, fewest, big, bigger, biggest, small, smaller, smallest, least, most

Compare, order –first, second, third etc.

Before, after, next, between

Measure

Length – metre, length, height, width, depth, deep, deeper, deepest, short, shorter, shortest, tall, taller, tallest, high ,higher, highest, low, lower, lowest, wide, narrow, thick, thin, thinner, thinnest, long, longer, longest, far, near, close

Weight – weigh, weighs, balances, heavy, heavier, heaviest, light, lighter, lightest, heavier than, lighter than, scales, more, less

Capacity – full, empty, half full, holds, container, more, less, nearly full, nearly empty, most, least

Time – time, days of the week, Monday, Tuesday etc., day, week, birthday, morning, afternoon, evening, night, bedtime, dinner time, playtime, today, yesterday, tomorrow, before, after, next, last, now, soon, early, late, quick, quicker, quickest, quickly, slow, slower, slowest, slowly, old, older, oldest, new, newer, newest, hour, o'clock, clock, watch, hands

Money – money, coin, penny, pence, pound, price, cost, buy, sell, spend, spent, pay

Shape and pattern	Curved, straight, round, hollow, solid, sort, make, build, draw, size, bigger, larger, smaller, symmetrical, pattern, repeating pattern, next, match, 2-D shape, corner, side, rectangle (including square), circle, triangle, 3-D shape, face, edge, vertex, vertices, cube, pyramid, sphere, cone

Position and direction	Position, over, under, above, below, top, bottom, side, on, in, outside, inside, around, in front, behind, front, back, beside, next to, opposite, apart, between, middle, edge, corner, direction, left, right, up, down, forwards, backwards, sideways, across, close, near, far, along, through, to, from, towards, away from, slide, move, roll, turn, stretch, bend, whole turn, half turn

General	Pattern, recognise, describe, compare, sort, count, group, list, find

Making Environments for Maths Measuring

Once again we come back to the environment being key to children developing good understanding of the concept of measuring. Children need access to lots of resources in lots of areas to enable them to be able to make comparisons (which is what measurements are). Measurement comes into so many of the children's everyday life experiences that we need to again make sure we are reflecting these in our settings. Even something as simple as threading washers onto bolts includes lots of length and width comparison as children build their fine motor skills. Block play offers a chance to compare size, width and weight of resources with a variety of blocks and loose parts. Even a box of dinosaurs can lead to talk of long necks, bigger teeth and smaller feet. The language of measure does not always need "measuring tools". If we enrich our environment with an array of "measuring tools" too, such as rulers, tape measures, scales and timers the maths potential extends even further. Referring to home elements such as TV guides, calendars and diaries leads to good play with an option to include the language of time. Using real tins and packets gives children a chance to talk about heavy and light whilst role playing. Using large equipment like builder's buckets, big spades and gravel outdoors helps children to really grasp the concept of heavy, whilst access to loads of sticks, pine cones and shells will offer opportunities for exploring length, size and weight.

Throughout this book, it has become increasingly apparent that maths potential sits within most well-resourced early years environments and that the key to good learning and understanding is in the practitioner's ability to spot what maths is happening in front of them as they play with and alongside the children. With this in mind the final section of the book looks to point out some of the maths potential within some of the most common areas of early years provision. It is by no means an exhaustive list – just a prompt for practitioners and hopefully some photographic inspiration when it comes to developing maths potential in your own settings.

Looking for Learning

Unlocking maths potential in early years requires us to both enable environments and to look for maths learning within children's play. In this section I will aim to highlight some of the enhancements you can add to some popular areas of provision to maximise maths potential, Also I will try to point out some of the maths learning you might see. Remember this is NOT about setting out an activity for children to "do", it is about enabling environments to have the best possible chance of children accessing maths as part of their own child led play.

Block Play

An essential for any early years setting, a good, well resourced block play area has so much potential for maths exploration as well as for problem solving, shared learning and critical thinking skills. Wherever possible I would recommend making your block play as open and accessible as possible and to enhance it with loose parts which can be added to any structures the children choose to create.

Resources: Wooden blocks in a wide variety of shapes and sizes, pine cones, tin cans in a variety of sizes (sharp edges sanded), mirrors, bricks, pebbles, shells, gems, bottle tops/lids, clear perspex sheets, cardboard roll, egg boxes, wooden discs, plumbing pipes, planks.

Look out for: Opportunities to talk about the shape of the blocks, the number of blocks being used to build with, the height, length, and width of constructions, pattern making with blocks and loose parts, positional language as children build (using blocks on, next to, behind etc.), comparison of shapes, colours and size, matching and sorting of shapes, shape language, reflections and symmetry if mirrors are used, lots of maths language such as more, less, higher, lower, bigger, smaller etc. and ways that shapes fit together to make bigger shapes and structures.

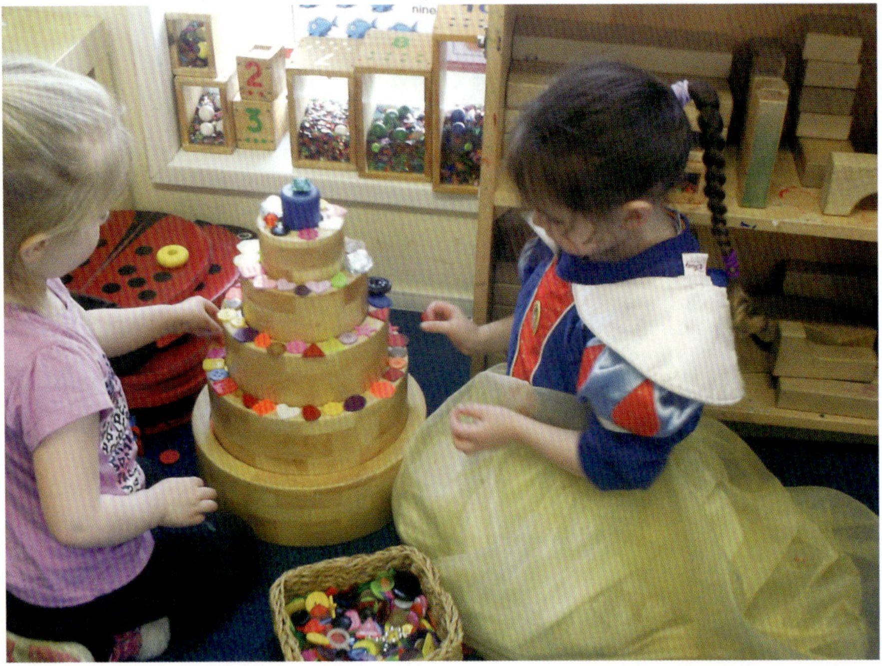

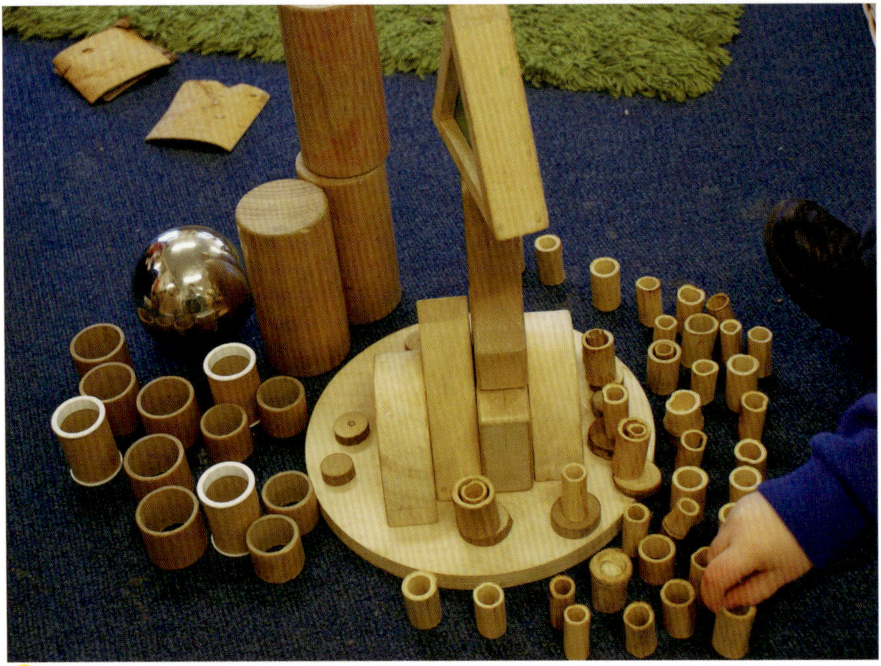

Investigation Station

Not an obvious area to look for maths but actually, if well stocked, it can offer loads of opportunities to explore and extend maths play.

Resources: Magnifiers, light panel, mirrors, torches, large selection of natural objects (pine cones, acorns, seeds, flowers, shells, insects, rocks, gems, coloured perspex, plants, magnetic shapes, nuts and bolts, textured materials such as wool, leather, straw etc. a variety of clocks and timers (electronic and sand).

Look out for: Focusing talk on shape and size when exploring objects, using language such as big, small, round, spiky, long, short, etc. counting natural objects, sorting and matching materials according to their shape, size and what they are made of, using magnifiers to explore textures and patterns on objects, looking for and talking about shapes in nature (spirals on shells, lines on leaves, petal shapes on flowers), Using magnifiers and binoculars to make things look bigger/smaller, exploring shapes and colours on a light panel sorting, matching and talking about the shapes, as well as loads of counting of loose parts and materials.

Role Play/Home Corner

One of the most powerful areas to resource for early maths, a home corner can hold so many opportunities for children to revisit maths that they meet every day. Don't forget to enhance your roleplay with all round maths opportunities, not just numbers.

Resources: Clocks, remote controls, calculators, mobile phones, egg timers, cookbooks, TV guides, calendars, computer keyboards, phone books, scales, crockery, storage tins of different sizes, real food packets and tins, purses with real money, dummy credit cards, real saucepans and utensils (give a real sense of weight), a wide selection of play or real food, baskets, shopping bags and handbags, spoons of differing sizes from very big to very small, sandtimers (for brushing teeth), thermometer (forehead one and one for room temp.) Toolbox with different sized spanners.

Look out for: Loads of weighing and comparisons with play food, talk about size with tins and saucepans, chances to talk about sharing, how many and do we have enough? Every day talk about familiar events and their order (dinner next, then bedtime etc.), talk about time from the clock and the calendar, numbers and numeral recognition on remotes, phones, recipes etc. Counting out with food or other items into bags, boxes etc. Talk about heavier and heaviest when using tins in the kitchen play. Chances to talk about 2 and 3D shapes with packets and tins and food. Language of capacity with filling or emptying saucepans, cups or bowls. Talk about money within shopping play as part of home play (rather than just a shop).

enable ... excite ... engage ... explore

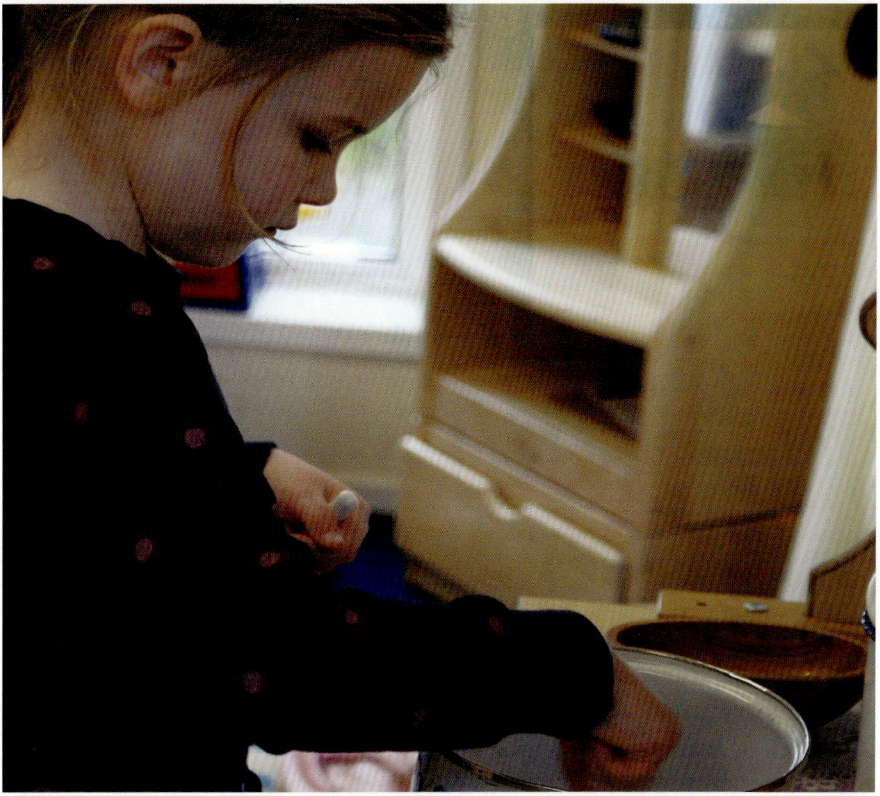

THANK YOU
Measuring
DONALD
0 1 2 3 4

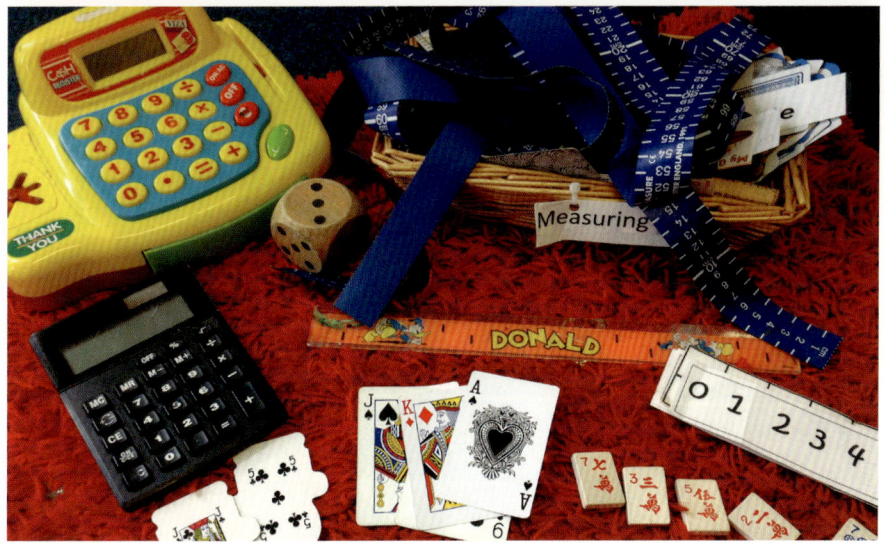

Indoor Loose Parts Play

Having access to a wide range of smaller loose parts can give rise to an amazing amount of maths potential. Remember to always risk assess and to supervise small parts use.

Resources: Plastics bottle lids (different colours and sizes), glass beads (various colours and shapes), curtain rings(wooden and metal), variety of buttons, cotton reels, lolly sticks (plain and coloured), bells, pegs, shells, polished pebbles, pine cones, matchsticks (plain and coloured), birthday cake candles, wooden sticks, nuts, bolts and washers.

Look out for: Lots of opportunities for sorting and matching according to size, shape and colour, patterns of colour, shape and number, counting sets of objects and counting out from a pile of objects, ordering thing from big to small, positional language like next, beside, on top etc., the opportunities to make shapes with the loose parts and to talk about the shapes, comparison language such as big, bigger, biggest, light, lighter, lightest.

Looking for Learning

Outdoor Loose Parts Play

Because outdoor learning is NOT indoor learning taken out through the door the loose parts on offer outdoors tend to be different either because of their size or because they are natural materials. These differences offer alternative opportunities for learning and therefore enhance indoor learning without replicating it.

enable ... excite ... engage ... explore

Resources: Milk crates, bread crates, planks, tyres (big and small), logs and logs slices, guttering and plastic pipe (different lengths), shells, pine cones, pebbles, sticks, bark, catkins, petals, fruit and veg, leaves, acorns, conkers,

Look out for: Lots of shapes in the crates, tyres etc. and for talk about shapes and size as children build structures with them. Positional language as they build structures or make assault courses (next to, on, under, through, behind etc.). Measurement language such as big, bigger, taller, wide, heavy etc. Counting small and large loose parts as they are moved, sorting and matching similar objects, looking for differences. Combining objects to make more. Sharing objects out with each other as we play. Sort and pattern natural materials according to shape, size, colour, length, weight, etc. Opportunities to weigh loose parts when they are gathered or are moved. Natural materials often offer opportunities to count in 2's, 3's etc. Talk about shapes and patterns within natural objects such as shells and conkers. Using loose parts to fill other containers gives great opportunities to talk about more, less, full and empty. Using smaller loose parts to make shapes and patterns and to talk about their characteristics.

Water Play

Most children are drawn to water play either indoors or outdoors and by thinking about some of the learning processes which can potentially develop as part of this play we can greatly increase our chances of spotting maths as they explore. Outdoor water play offers opportunities to use much bigger equipment and hence explore full and heavy concepts on a much bigger scale and with whole body sensory experiences.

Resources: Funnels of different sizes, clear containers and bottles of varying sizes, pipes and guttering of differing lengths, shower pipes, metal bowls of a variety of sizes, tubing, spoons, scoops, sieves, turkey basters, syringes (small and large), shells, pebbles, water beads, bottle tops, corks, water wheels, metal gravy boats, metal jugs, buckets in wide variety of sizes (include extra large builders buckets and pails if possible).

Look out for: Obviously pouring offers lots of chances to model and explore the language of capacity and volume with talk of full, empty, more, less etc. Also watch out for chances to talk about the equipment children are using to explore the water with talk of big, bigger, biggest, long, long, longest, heavy, heavier etc. chances to sort additions such as shells, corks and pebbles according to colour, shape, size and weight as well as potentially exploring patterns if you have a platform to work on (a bath tray across your water tray is great for this).

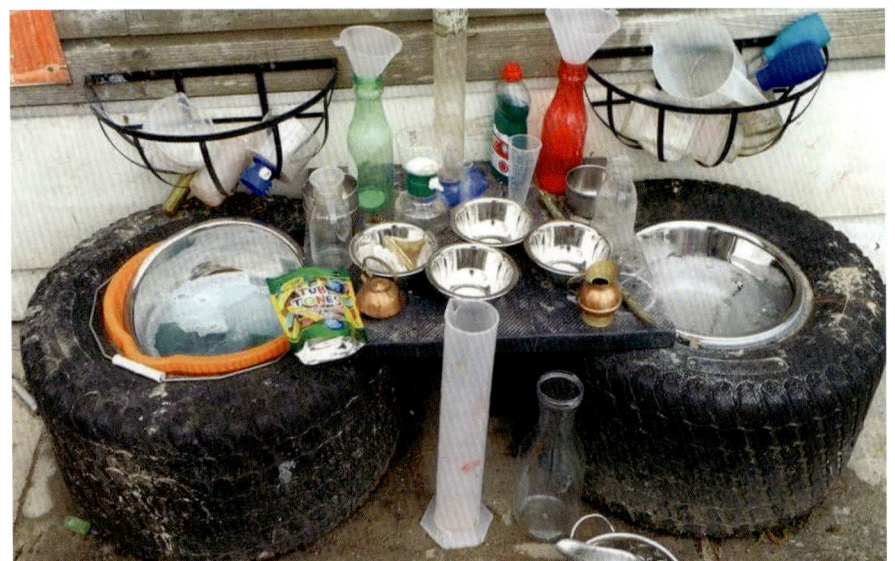

Sand Play

Sand play can give uniquely different opportunities for exploration, dependent on whether it is indoors or outdoors. Indoor sand tends to give more fine motor and texture explorations with sand often dry and more easily poured than wet sand. Outdoors sand can give access to scooping and pouring on a massive, whole body scale (space allowing) and goes hand in hand with gross motor development. Resourcing our sand play with multi-sensory equipment rather than just plastic allows for lots more brain firing and rewiring to occur.

Resources (indoors): Lots of "Treasure to Measure" – spoons (different sizes and lengths), sieves (different sizes), metal cups, scoops, plates, jelly moulds, egg cups, plates (different metals in a variety of colours). Loose parts such as coins, jewels and beads, bottle and jar lids, tubes and funnels.

Resources (outdoors): Larger scale equipment including big buckets, scoops and trowels, sieves (various sizes), lots of containers made from different materials and a variety of sizes, natural loose parts (sticks, pine cones, conkers, leaves, shells, acorns, wood slices, etc.), spoons of different sizes, socks of different sizes.

Look out for: Alongside all the physical fine and gross motor development and the scientific exploration of sand as a material and how it looks, feels and behaves, there are loads of opportunities for counting loose parts, scoops and handfuls. The opportunities for capacity language are clear with lots of full, empty, more and less to be modelled. With socks and other objects to fill and explore there is extended chances to explore the language and concept of length, size and weight first hand (long, longer, big, bigger, heavy and really heavy), loose parts additions will offer additional patterning, sorting and counting opportunities as well as shape. Exploring what fits inside what will help children develop their sense of spatial awareness.

enable ... excite ... engage ... explore

Mud Kitchen

An essential part of any good early years provision, a well equipped mud kitchen offers loads of learning opportunities across the curriculum including maths.

Resources: Lots of metal and wooden containers including bowls, jugs, saucepans, spoons, ladels, pestle and mortar, casserole dishes and cupcake baking trays. Access to an array of things to add to the mud creations including herbs, flowers, pebbles and other loose parts, fruit and vegetables and of course lots of mud and water.

Look our for: In exploring and creating their own recipes children will naturally explore capacity first hand as they fill or empty saucepans, cups and plates. Encourage capacity language such as empty, full, more and less and well as one more scoop, one less mint leaf or stone in the magic soup. By creating their own recipes children explore counting as they work out how many of each ingredient they want included. Access to a mud supply can offer a great chance to explore weight with cups and saucepans being heavy or light. Including loose parts such as petals, pebbles and pinecones give the added bonus of lots of shape, pattern and counting opportunities as children decorate or add to their creations. The addition of cupcake baking trays lends itself to natural counting and sharing of materials and ingredients.

Playdough Bar

In a child led environment where children have open access to a self service playdough facility as part of their ongoing fine motor development can hold huge potential for mathematical exploration and inquiry.

Resources: Lots of loose parts such as sticks, glass gems, wood chips, cake candles (stick and numeral varieties, cutters of various shapes, rollers of different textures, a selection of textured materials such a sand paper, bubble wrap, bark, artificial grass etc., scissors, knives (safe child versions), lolly sticks, herbs, pine cones, pebbles, etc.

Look out for: Because of the tactile nature of the playdough, free access allows the children to create their own shapes, to make long and short rolls of dough, to make patterns in the playdough with the textures, to count, match and sort the loose parts, to explore bigger and smaller pieces as well as building on an understanding of more, less and heavier and lighter. Usually a popular early years activity playdough play naturally explores concepts of sharing and division between friends. Adding self make facilities adds an extra dimension with the chance to build on capacity language and understanding such as more, less and how many scoops etc.

Cookery

Even in child led environments there is opportunity to use cookery and baking to develop maths skills and understanding. The key as ever is to let the children lead the way with what they want to make and then to look for the opportunities to talk about size, weight, sharing, language such as more, less, full, empty, how many?. Having balance scales can help children to explore heavier, lighter, more and less. Children can eventually follow the balance method to bake cakes which as well as measuring inquiry helps with sharing and counting skills too.

Balance cake method

Place 2 or three eggs on one side of the balance scales. Now balance the scales with equal amounts of self raising flour, butter or margarine and castor sugar. Add all of the ingredients to a bowl and mix thoroughly. Add the mixture to cake cases and bake until golden brown and risen.

Conclusion

So, as we have discovered throughout this book, the way to maximise access to mathematics skills, knowledge and understanding is through careful enabling of our environments and through sensitive interaction from adults. It is clear to see that for great maths potential to be unlocked the setting as a whole has to be developed, including physical access to resources and opportunities as well as staff confidence. Access to staff training is essential to build confident practitioners who are happy to play with and alongside children and to look for the maths within their play. Our goal has to be to develop adults and children alike who understand the importance and usefulness of maths in everyday life.

It is clear that maths does not exist as a stand alone subject. It is central to and intertwined with so many other aspects of learning. The characteristics of effective learning apply equally to maths as they do to any area of early years development. Building good quality, well resourced, open ended environments for children to explore and build on their own ideas and thinking will lead just as much to good quality maths as it will to other learning. We just have to learn to look for the learning and follow the children with what they know rather than what we think they should know. Let the children guide you through their world, don't force our world upon them.

Conclusion